FROM ISLAM TO CHRISTIAN

RELIGIOUS FESTIVALS FROM AROUND THE WORLD
RELIGION FOR KIDS
CHILDREN'S RELIGION BOOKS

BABY PROFESSOR
EDUCATION KIDS

Speedy Publishing LLC
40 E. Main St. #1156
Newark, DE 19711
www.speedypublishing.com
Copyright 2017

All Rights reserved. No part of this book may be reproduced or used in any way or form or by any means whether electronic or mechanical, this means that you cannot record or photocopy any material ideas or tips that are provided in this book.

In this book, we're going to talk all about religious festivals around the world. So, let's get right to it!

Every religion has special feasts, festivals, and holidays to commemorate important religious events.

January

M	T	W	T	F	S	S
1	2	3	4	5	6	7
8	9	10	11	12	13	14
15	16	17	18	19	20	21
22	23	24	25	26	27	28
29	30	31				

February

M	T	W	T	F	S	S
			1	2	3	4
5	6	7	8	9	10	11
12	13	14	15	16	17	18
19	20	21	22	23	24	25
26	27	28				

March

M	T	W	T	F	S	S
		1	2	3	4	
5	6	7	8	9	10	11
12	13	14	15	16	17	18
19	20	21	22	23	24	25
26	27	28	29	30	31	

April

M	T	W	T	F	S	S
						1
2	3	4	5	6	7	8
9	10	11	12	13	14	15
16	17	18	19	20	21	22
23	24	25	26	27	28	29
30						

May

M	T	W	T	F	S	S
1	2	3	4	5	6	
7	8	9	10	11	12	13
14	15	16	17	18	19	20
21	22	23	24	25	26	27
28	29	30	31			

June

M	T	W	T	F	S	S
			1	2	3	
4	5	6	7	8	9	10
11	12	13	14	15	16	17
18	19	20	21	22	23	24
25	26	27	28	29	30	

July

M	T	W	T	F	S	S
					1	
2	3	4	5	6	7	8
9	10	11	12	13	14	15
16	17	18	19	20	21	22
23	24	25	26	27	28	29
30	31					

August

M	T	W	T	F	S	S
	1	2	3	4	5	
6	7	8	9	10	11	12
13	14	15	16	17	18	19
20	21	22	23	24	25	26
27	28	29	30	31		

September

M	T	W	T	F	S	S
				1	2	
3	4	5	6	7	8	9
10	11	12	13	14	15	16
17	18	19	20	21	22	23
24	25	26	27	28	29	30

October

M	T	W	T	F	S	S
1	2	3	4	5	6	7
8	9	10	11	12	13	14
15	16	17	18	19	20	21
22	23	24	25	26	27	28
29	30	31				

November

M	T	W	T	F	S	S
		1	2	3	4	
5	6	7	8	9	10	11
12	13	14	15	16	17	18
19	20	21	22	23	24	25
26	27	28	29	30		

December

M	T	W	T	F	S	S
				1	2	
3	4	5	6	7	8	9
10	11	12	13	14	15	16
17	18	19	20	21	22	23
24	25	26	27	28	29	30
31						

IMPORTANT ISLAMIC HOLIDAYS

In the western world, we follow a type of calendar known as the Gregorian calendar. The Islamic calendar is different. They also have 12 months, but their calendar is based on the phases of the moon so each month has at least 29 and at most 30 days.

Therefore, their calendar usually only has either 354 or 355 total days, instead of the 365 days in the Gregorian calendar. Because of the changing schedule of the moon, the dates of their holidays move each year, so they have no set dates.

Mai

19	20	21	22
16	23	30	
17	24	31	
25			
26			

Juni

Woche	22	23	24	25	26
Mo		6	13	20	27
Di		7	14	21	28
Mi	1	8	15	22	29
Do	2	9	16	23	30
Fr	3	10	17	24	
Sa	4	11	18	25	
So	**5**	**12**	**19**	**26**	

August

	31	32	33	34	35
	1	8	15		

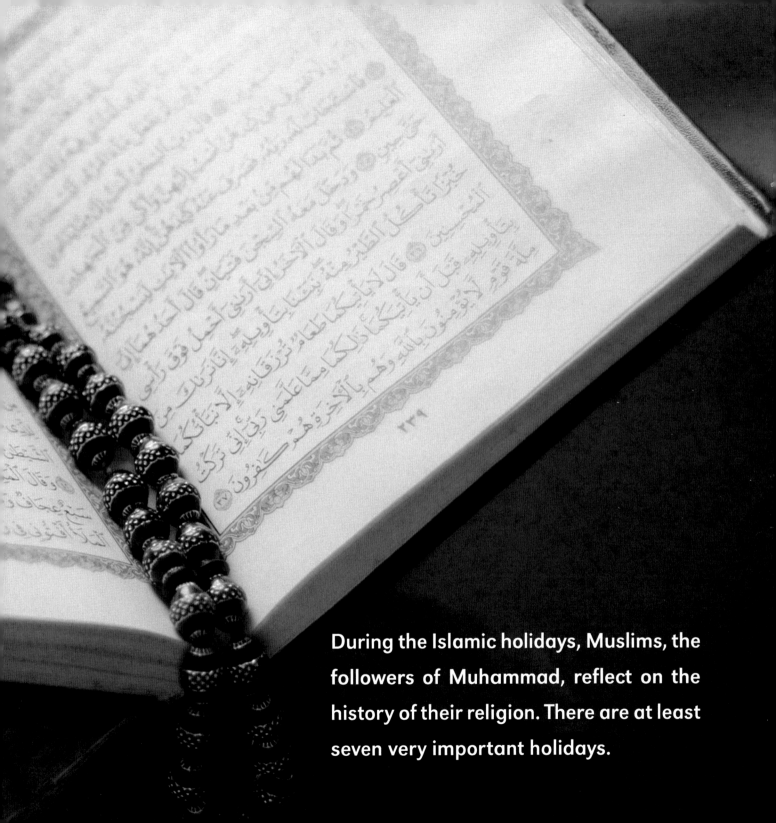

During the Islamic holidays, Muslims, the followers of Muhammad, reflect on the history of their religion. There are at least seven very important holidays.

AL HIJRAH

This holiday is the celebration of the New Year. It takes place on the very first day of the first month of the year, which is called Muharram. Sometimes the holiday is just called "Muharram" after this first month of the year.

On this day, Muslims celebrate when the prophet Muhammad and those who believed in his teachings went on a journey from the holy city of Mecca to the city of Medina. Muslim people spend this important day worshipping and spending time reflecting and praying.

ASHURA

On the tenth day of the first month of the year, called Muharram, Muslims have a day where they fast. This religious holiday is called Ashura.

MAWLID AN NABI

The third month of the year is called Rabi al-Awwal. On the 12th day of this month, the day Muhammad was born is celebrated. This holiday is called Mawlid an Nabi. People celebrate with parades and singing to commemorate his birth.

RAMADAN

The ninth month of the year in their calendar is known as Ramadan. This is a very holy month for Muslims because they believe that it is the month that Muhammad received the words for the holy book called the Quran. During this month, they often read the entire text of the Quran, which has over 6,000 verses. They also abstain from eating and drinking from dawn to sunset. They can eat before and after, but they can't even have a sip of water from dawn to sunset.

THE HOLY QUR'AN

Translation and commentary
by
A. YUSUF ALI

Published by
Islamic Propagation Centre
International

Not everyone has to fast during Ramadan. Young children, people who are too old or sick, and women who are pregnant don't always fast during Ramadan. At the end of the month of Ramadan, Muslim people give gifts to those who are impoverished. The gift they give is known as "Zakat."

LAYLAT AL-QADR

Laylat al-Qadr occurs during the end of the month of the Ramadan celebration. It is also sometimes described as the "Night of Power." During this holy day, Muslims remember the important night when Allah, the Muslim God, began to present the holy word to Muhammad in the form of the Quran. This occurred over twenty-three years.

EID AL-FITR

The word "Eid" translates to festival. This religious holiday is a very important one and marks the conclusion of Ramadan. It is the first day of the 10th month of the year, which is known as Shawwal. During this time, families who are Muslim gather to eat meals together and to give gifts to each other.

EID AL-ADHA

The festival called Eid al Adha is the most important of the Islamic religious holidays. It starts on the 10th day of the 12th month of the year, which is called Dhu al-Hijjah. The festival concludes on the 13th day of the month.

This religious holiday celebrates the event where Abraham was going to kill his beloved son Isaac because God commanded that he do so. Abraham is thought to be the father of all three major religions that believe in one God–Islam, Judaism, and Christianity. God didn't let Abraham kill his son, but it was important that Abraham was willing to do so. On this religious holiday, Muslim families share meals, offer animal sacrifices to God, and exchange gifts.

IMPORTANT JEWISH HOLIDAYS

Like the Islamic calendar, the Jewish calendar for religious holidays is also based on the phases of the moon, so the dates of their religious celebrations vary within a span of days from year to year. All of their holidays begin when the sun sets on the day they start.

ROSH HASHANAH

Rosh Hashanah celebrates two events. It celebrates God's creation of the world and it also marks the New Year for Jewish people. It's celebrated 163 days after the holiday of Passover. It does NOT occur on Sunday, or Friday, or Wednesday, but it can fall on the dates between the 5th of September and the 5th of October.

This important holiday is a time for Jewish people to reflect on their lives and pray. A shofar, which is a type of horn, is blown to officially begin the New Year. One hundred notes are blown on the shofar each day. Jewish people send each other cards and they often have celebratory gatherings as well. This holiday has been commemorated for thousands of years and there are many traditional foods that are eaten including a braided, egg bread known as challah and sweets, such as honey and apples.

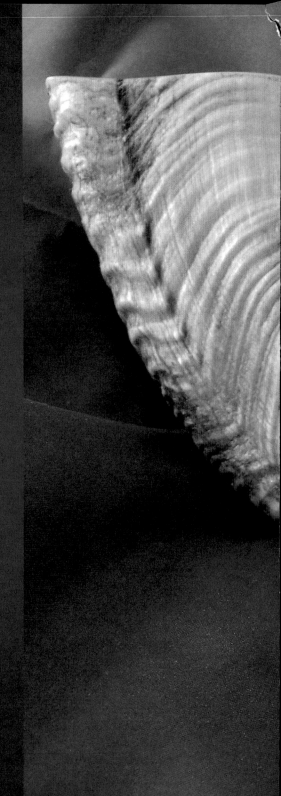

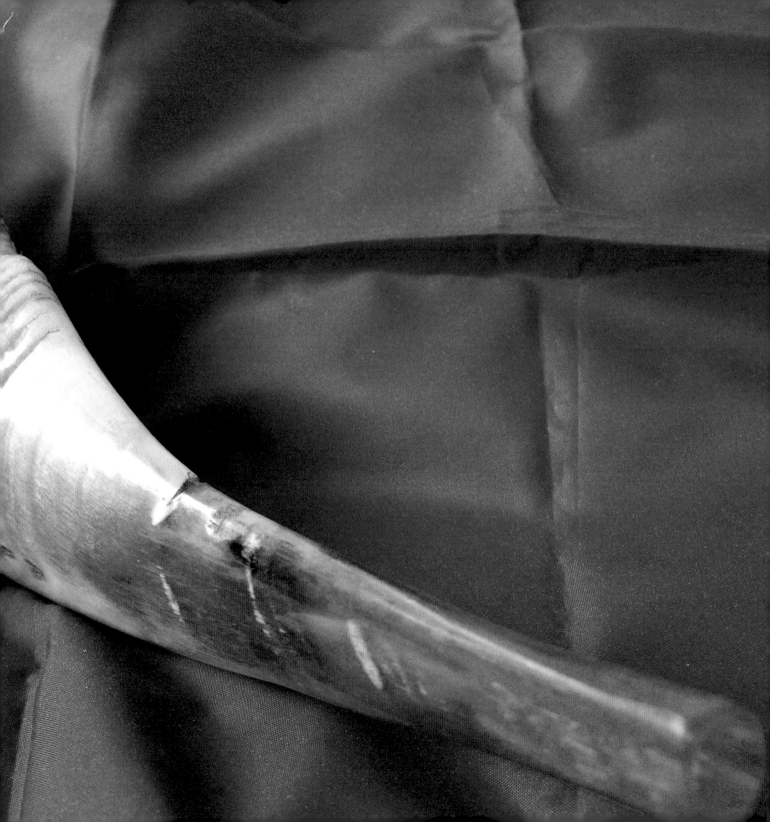

TASHLIKH

Some Jewish people participate in Tashlikh, which is a water ceremony similar to baptism. People walk into a body of water to erase their sins. They empty their pockets, which have bread pieces in them, to signify that they are making themselves clean and free from sin.

PASSOVER

Passover is one of the main Jewish religious holidays. During this holiday, the Jewish people remember the time when the Israelites were freed from their slavery in Egypt and led to the Promised Land by their leader Moses. This holiday has been celebrated since 1300 BC, as God commanded. Passover lasts for seven or eight days and it occurs in the Jewish month of Nissan, which is in March or April, so it is often close to the Christian holiday of Easter.

God sent ten plagues so the Egyptians would release the Jewish people from slavery. For the tenth plague, the angel of death came from house to house to kill the firstborn children. To make sure that the Jewish homes would be passed over, they put blood from a lamb above their doors. Unleavened bread is eaten during Passover to commemorate the fact that the Jewish people had to leave Egypt so quickly that their bread didn't have time to rise.

YOM KIPPUR

Yom Kippur is a very important Jewish holiday. It's known as the most important holy day for Jewish people. It's celebrated ten days after the holiday of Rosh Hashanah. This means that Yom Kippur is observed during September or October. The reason this day is commemorated is because it is the day when Jewish people ask God for the forgiveness of their sins. There are five services with prayers that take place throughout the day. Many Jewish people fast for a period of 25 hours during Yom Kippur. It is a serious religious holiday.

YOM KIPPUR

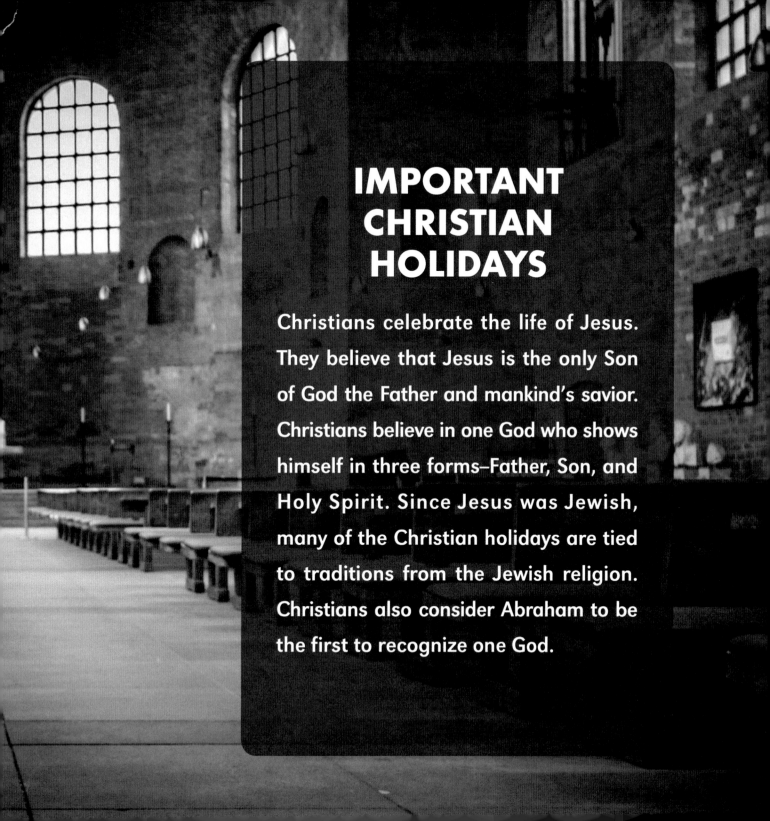

IMPORTANT CHRISTIAN HOLIDAYS

Christians celebrate the life of Jesus. They believe that Jesus is the only Son of God the Father and mankind's savior. Christians believe in one God who shows himself in three forms–Father, Son, and Holy Spirit. Since Jesus was Jewish, many of the Christian holidays are tied to traditions from the Jewish religion. Christians also consider Abraham to be the first to recognize one God.

CHRISTMAS DAY

No one knows exactly what day Jesus Christ was born. Because of this, the first Christian church leaders selected that day to commemorate his birth. The first time the date is mentioned is in a document from 354 AD.

Jesus was born in a lowly stable and placed in a manger by his mother Mary. Christians believe that Jesus is God's son. He died to atone for mankind's sins. He suffered a terrible death on a cross, even though he was innocent of any crime.

There are many different aspects to the Christmas holiday. It is a religious holiday and celebrated in churches throughout the world. It has also become a time when many people exchange gifts, decorate a tree, and sing songs, some religious and some not. Many non-Christians love this holiday of peace and joy as well.

EASTER

Easter commemorates the resurrection of Jesus into heaven, three days after his death. Unlike Christmas, Easter is not celebrated on the same day every year. Because Jesus's resurrection occurred around the time of the Jewish Passover, the date varies based on this. However, its date is usually the very first Sunday after the occurrence of the full moon, on or after the spring equinox, which happens in March.

The equinox is when the sun's rays hit the equator directly and the length of day and night are almost the same. In any case, Easter occurs between March and May, although there have been proposals for changing the way the date is determined since it is rather complicated. Easter is celebrated with religious ceremonies. It is a time of family gatherings and festive food after the fasting of the Lent season.

DIFFERENT, BUT SIMILAR

All three religions of Islam, Judaism, and Christianity considered Abraham as their father. The holidays of these three major religions have been celebrated for thousands of years. Some holidays include meals and merriment, but others are mostly fasting and religious ceremonies.

Awesome! Now that you've read all about religious festivals around the world, you may want to read about December holidays in the Baby Professor book December Holidays from Around the World.

Visit

BABY PROFESSOR
EDUCATION KIDS

www.BabyProfessorBooks.com

to download Free Baby Professor eBooks
and view our catalog of new and exciting
Children's Books

Made in the USA
Columbia, SC
05 October 2021

46707363R00038